NATIONAL GEOGRAPHIC KiDS

weird but true! 7

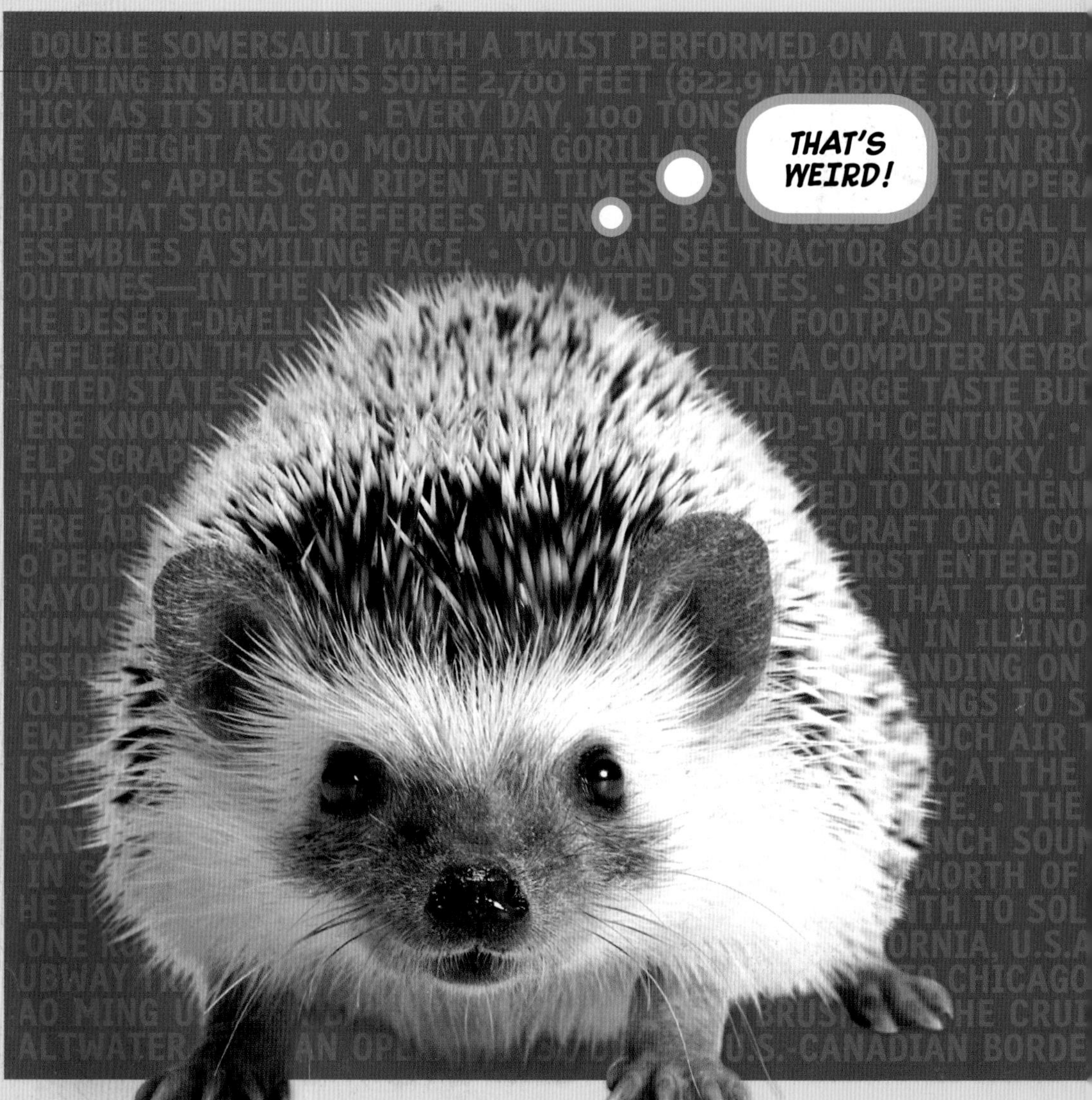
THAT'S WEIRD!

NATIONAL
GEOGRAPHIC
KiDS

weird but true! 7

300 outrageous facts

NATIONAL GEOGRAPHIC
WASHINGTON, D.C.

NEW
YORKE

4

On average, the **Empire State Building** in New York City .is hit by

lightning

25 times a year.

AN ITALIAN DESIGNER MADE A COUCH SHAPED LIKE A CHOCOLATE BAR.

RED-FOOTED TORTOISES HAVE BEEN TAUGHT TO USE TOUCH SCREENS.

Sitting in a **cardboard box** can lower **stress** for **domestic cats.**

6

Your brain makes up only **2 percent** of your total body weight but uses up to **20 percent** of your body's energy.

HONEYBEES
HAVE
TWO
STOMACHS.

Some
frogs
have
green
bones.

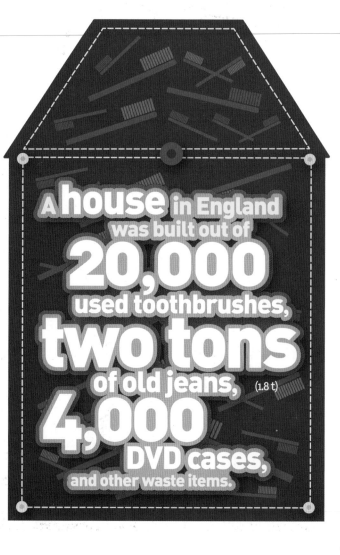

A **house** in England
was built out of
20,000
used toothbrushes,
two tons
of old jeans, (1.8 t)
4,000
DVD cases,
and other waste items.

GOLDEN ORB-WEAVING SPIDERS THAT LIVE IN CITIES GROW BIGGER THAN ONES IN RURAL AREAS.

SARCASTIC
FRINGEHEAD FISH
BATTLE
OVER TURF BY
WRESTLING
EACH OTHER WITH
THEIR MOUTHS.

THE HEAVIEST **CAULIFLOWER** ON RECORD WEIGHED MORE **THAN A BULLDOG.**

UP TO HALF OF THE WATER ON EARTH IS OLDER THAN THE SUN, ACCORDING TO ONE STUDY.

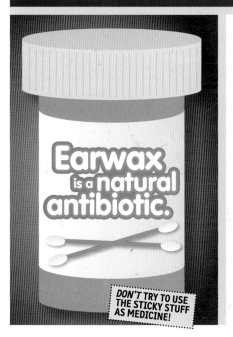

Earwax is a natural antibiotic.

DON'T TRY TO USE THE STICKY STUFF AS MEDICINE!

Food travels through your esophagus at a speed of about one inch (2.5 cm) a second.

3,000,000,000

MORE THAN **THREE BILLION** PASSENGERS TRAVEL ON COMMERCIAL AIRPLANES EVERY YEAR.

A STUDY FOUND THAT **CHEWING GUM** PUTS YOU IN A **BETTER MOOD.**

ONE MAN INVENTED **A SUPERFAST POTATO PEELER** OUT OF A TOILET BRUSH ATTACHED TO A DRILL.

A SPANISH SCIENTIST INVENTED **ICE CREAM** THAT **CHANGES COLORS** WHEN **LICKED.**

THE PUDU— A SMALL KIND OF DEER— RUNS IN A ZIGZAG PATTERN TO ESCAPE PREDATORS.

YOU HAVE **TASTE RECEPTORS** IN YOUR STOMACH.

SPITTING SPIDERS IMMOBILIZE **PREY** BY **SPRAYING** THEM WITH **POISONOUS** FLUID.

It takes more than **ten** gallons (38 L) of water to make one slice of bread.

The average wait time at a **fast-food** burger restaurant drive-through is **203 seconds.**

Cockroaches
that lived **250 million years ago** were as big as today's **house cats.**

23

ARTIST CHARLES M. SCHULZ CREATED NEARLY 18,000 "PEANUTS" COMIC STRIPS.

Some airplane pilots use a beach on Fraser Island, Australia, as a landing strip.

Scientists have found a way to return hard-boiled egg whites to liquid form.

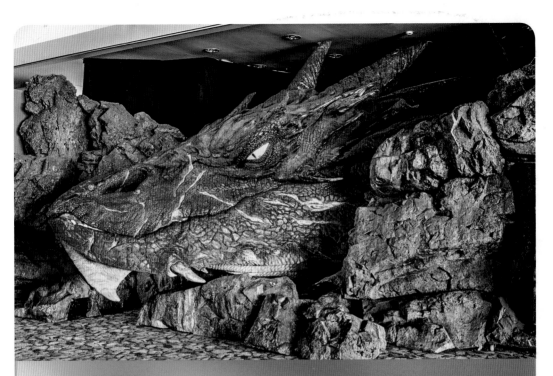

PASSENGERS ARRIVING AT ONE **NEW ZEALAND AIRPORT** ARE GREETED BY A **14-FOOT BUST** OF THE **DRAGON** (4.3-m) **Smaug** FROM *THE HOBBIT* MOVIE TRILOGY.

Scientists think that the center of the moon may be SQUISHY.

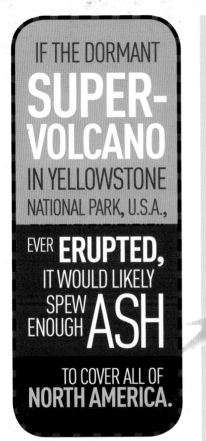

IF THE DORMANT **SUPER-VOLCANO** IN YELLOWSTONE NATIONAL PARK, U.S.A., EVER **ERUPTED,** IT WOULD LIKELY SPEW ENOUGH **ASH** TO COVER ALL OF **NORTH AMERICA.**

The **Pac-Man frog** can lift three times its own **body weight** with its tongue.

LISTENING TO **CLASSICAL MUSIC** CAN HELP **DOGS RELAX,** A STUDY FOUND.

A DUTCH
COMPANY
PLANS TO BUILD A
**SNOWFLAKE-
SHAPED HOTEL**
THAT FLOATS
ON **WATER.**

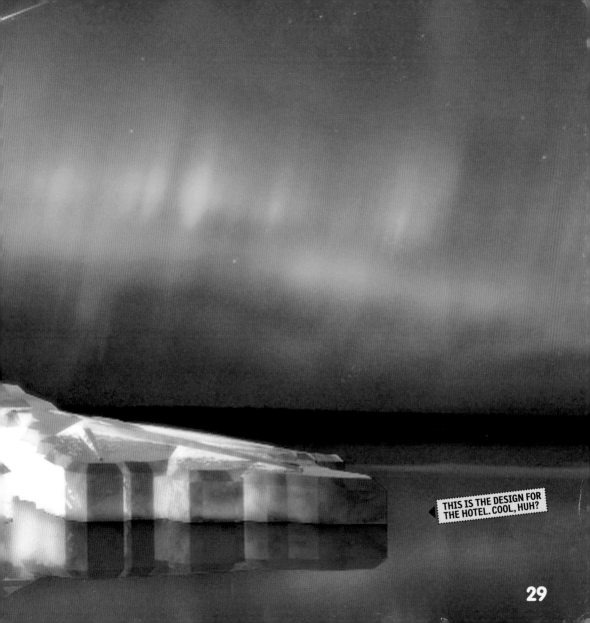

THIS IS THE DESIGN FOR
THE HOTEL. COOL, HUH?

A NEWSPAPER IN SRI LANKA

was printed with insect-repelling ink to keep readers from getting bug bites.

HUMANS AND KATYDIDS

SAY WHAT?

HAVE SIMILARLY STRUCTURED

EARS.

THE GIANT **PITCHER PLANT** SECRETES **NECTAR** TO LURE BUGS AND RODENTS INTO ITS **"MOUTH."**

31

A SOUTH KOREAN BASEBALL TEAM INSTALLED **CHEERING ROBOTS** IN THE STANDS OF ITS BALLPARK.

A record **232 people** did a **cannonball dive all at once** into a harbor in New Zealand.

ONE KIND OF **MUSHROOM** RESEMBLES A **HUMAN BRAIN.**

Between 1886 and 1902, the *Statue of Liberty* was used as a lighthouse.

Humans may have once had a third eyelid.

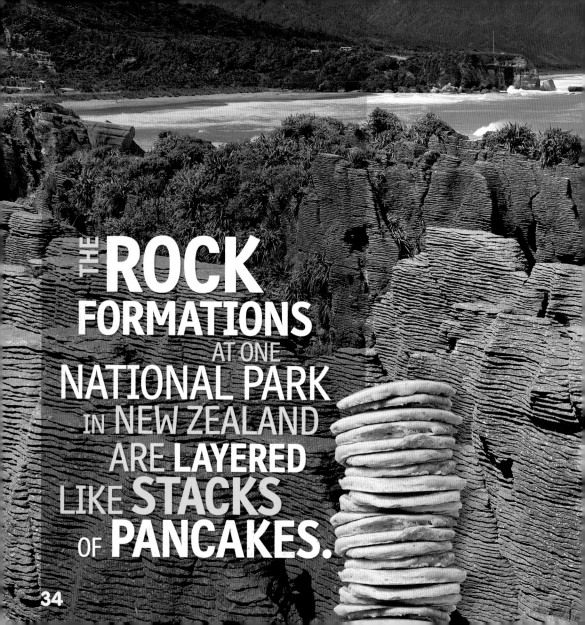

THE **ROCK FORMATIONS** AT ONE **NATIONAL PARK** IN **NEW ZEALAND** ARE **LAYERED** LIKE **STACKS** OF **PANCAKES.**

GIANT CUTTLEFISH HAVE BAGEL-SHAPED BRAINS.

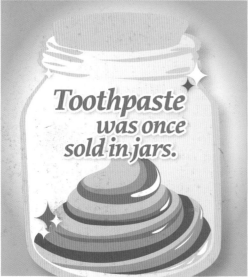

Toothpaste was once sold in jars.

During the **Ice Age,** supersize **Lions** roamed what is now the United Kingdom.

HUMMINGBIRDS FLAP THEIR WINGS UP TO 80 TIMES A SECOND.

IT WOULD TAKE A SPACESHIP ABOUT 450 MILLION YEARS TO REACH THE EDGE OF OUR GALAXY.

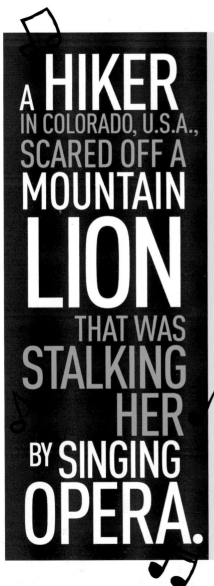

A **HIKER** IN COLORADO, U.S.A., SCARED OFF A **MOUNTAIN LION** THAT WAS STALKING HER BY SINGING **OPERA.**

A KIND OF **BIRD** THAT LIVED 25 MILLION YEARS AGO HAD A **WINGSPAN** LONGER THAN SIX BASEBALL **BATS.**

39

SOME RAINBOWS APPEAR TO

CONTAIN ONLY SHADES OF RED.

About **6,000 hours** of new videos are posted to **YouTube** every hour.

42

You don't **sneeze** while you're sleeping.

ONE **WOMAN** **WALKED** **10,000** **MILES** (16,093 km) ACROSS ASIA AND AUSTRALIA IN THREE YEARS.

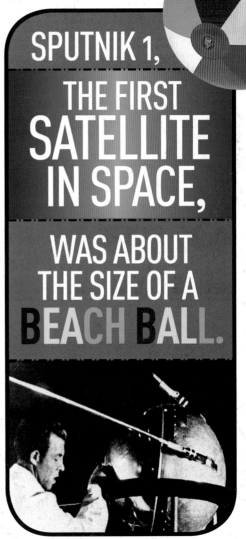

SPUTNIK 1, THE FIRST **SATELLITE** IN SPACE, WAS ABOUT THE SIZE OF A BEACH BALL.

43

At an annual race in Totnes, England, competitors kick **oranges** along the course as they run.

44

On average, a **$1 bill** is in circulation in the United States for about **six years.**

item sold on eBay was a broken laser pointer.

A **cobra** bit a chef in China **20** minutes

AFTER its head had been CUT from its body.

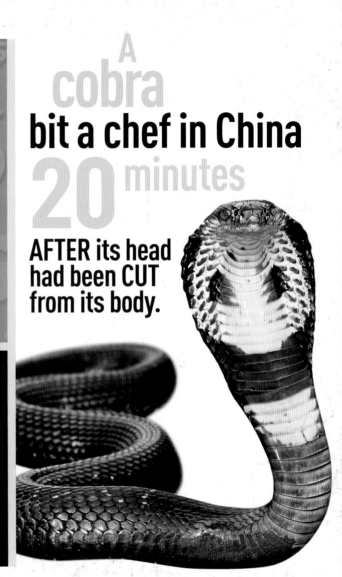

EACH YEAR,
WINDS BLOW ABOUT
40 MILLION
TONS OF DUST
FROM AFRICA'S (36 million t)
SAHARA ...

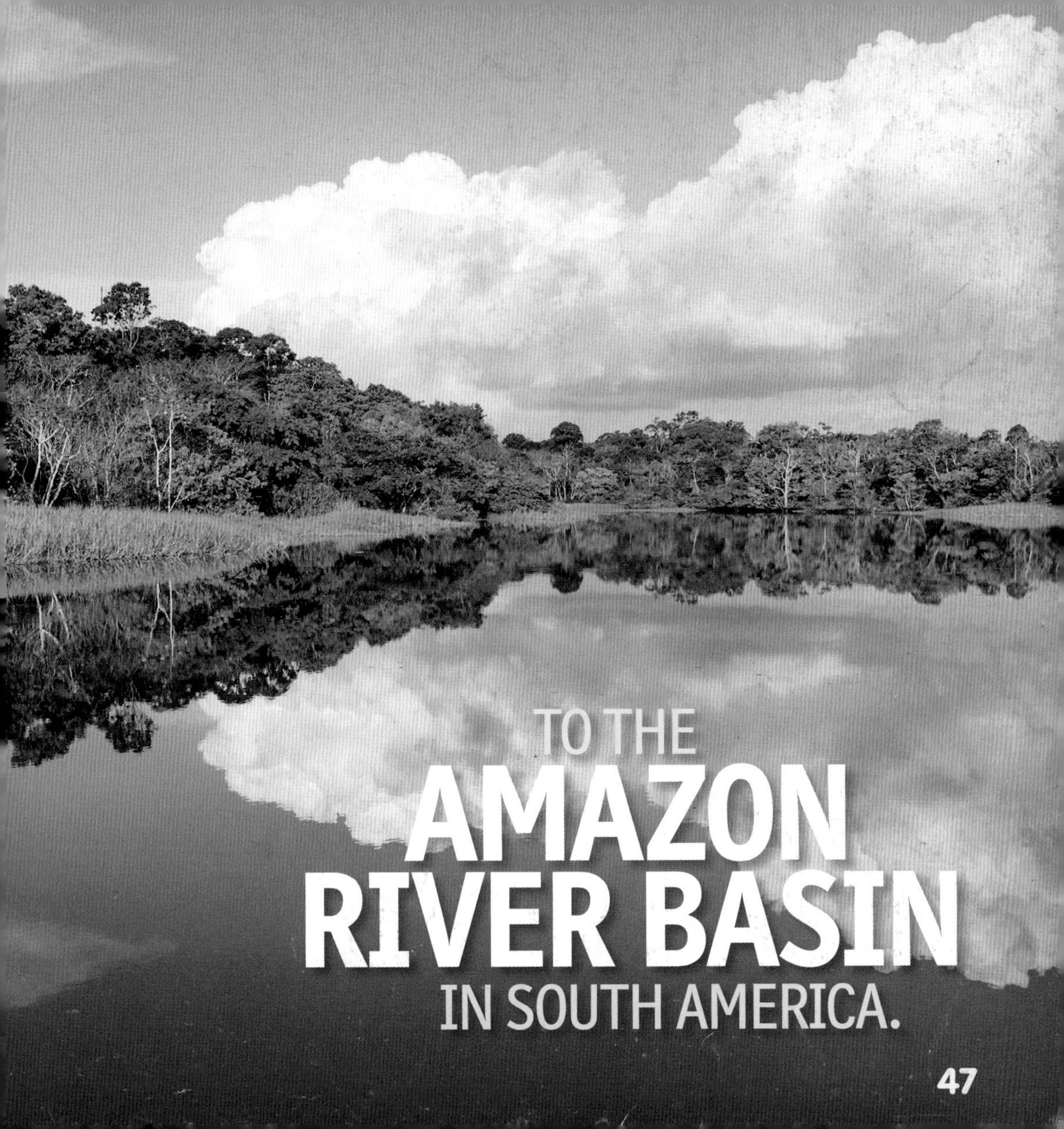

TO THE
**AMAZON
RIVER BASIN**
IN SOUTH AMERICA.

There are more than 20,000 TV stations in the world.

FOUND IN
AUSTRALIA AND
NEW GUINEA, THE
**SOUTHERN
CASSOWARY
BIRD**
HAS CLAWS NEARLY
THE LENGTH
OF AN iPHONE.

The **coati,**
a member of
the raccoon family,
can rotate its ankles
180 degrees.

When reading, you blink about half as much as usual.

MORE THAN
29,000
GRAINS ARE IN A
ONE-POUND (0.5-kg)
BAG OF RICE.

A **HEXAGON-SHAPED HURRICANE** HAS HOVERED OVER SATURN'S NORTH POLE FOR AT LEAST **30 YEARS.**

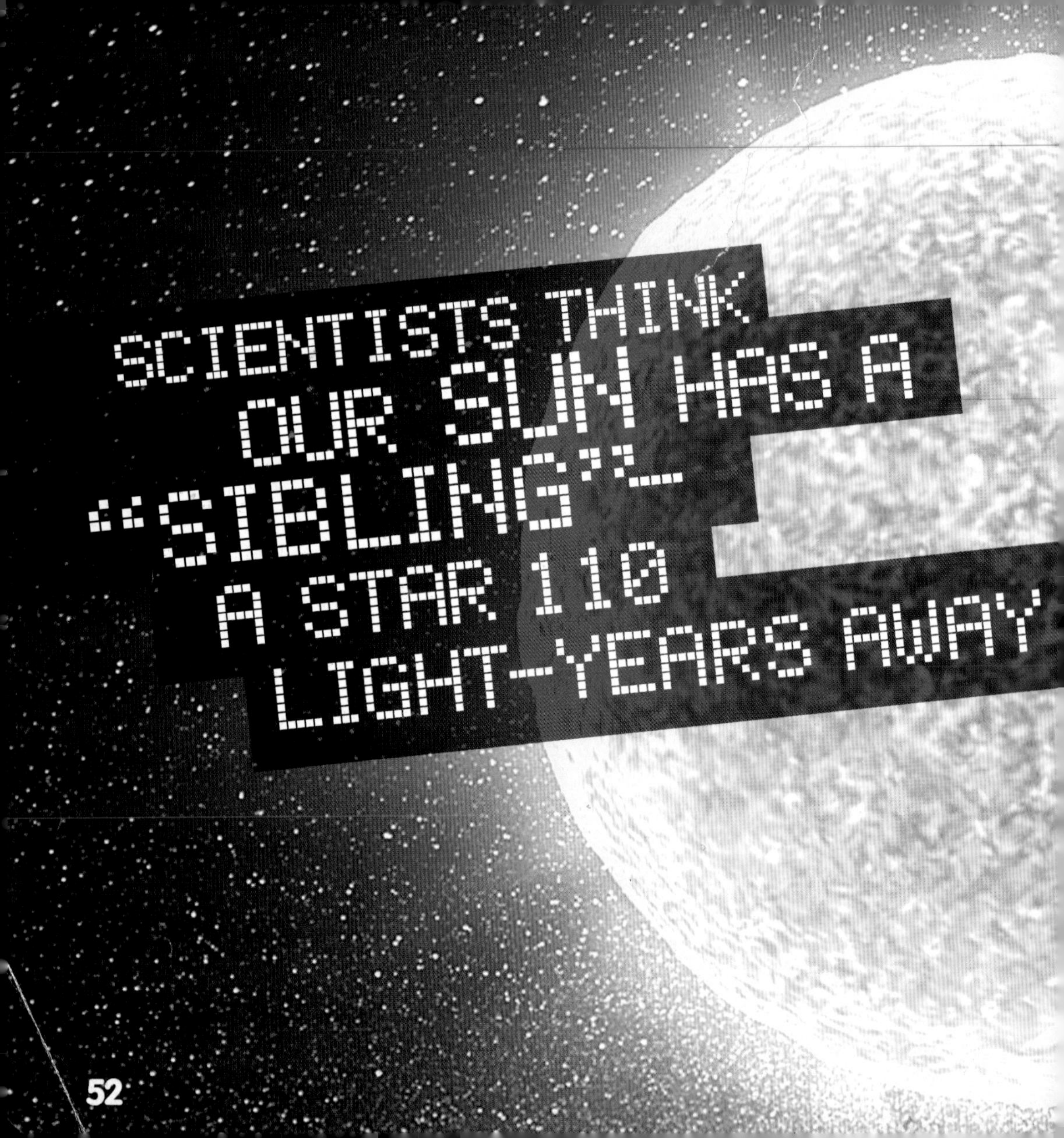

SCIENTISTS THINK OUR SUN HAS A "SIBLING"— A STAR 110 LIGHT-YEARS AWAY

THAT WAS BORN FROM THE SAME ANCIENT GAS CLOUD.

ILLUSTRATION OF THE SUN'S SIBLING STAR AND AN ORBITING PLANET

A group of **Twitter** users in Japan once posted **143,199** tweets in **one** second.

A STUDY FOUND THAT THE LONGER YOU SLEEP, THE StRANGEr YOUR DREAMS BECOME.

VOLCANOES ONCE ERUPTED ON THE MOON.

Hello Kitty's full name is Kitty White.

LIFTING WEIGHTS

MAY IMPROVE YOUR MEMORY.

A
FRESHWATER LAKE
THE SIZE OF LAKE ONTARIO
IS HIDDEN UNDER NEARLY
2.5 MILES OF ICE
(4 km) IN ANTARCTICA.

More **American cash** is spent **outside** the **United States** than inside its borders.

At the **Starbucks** in CIA headquarters, in Virginia, U.S.A., workers aren't allowed to **write** customers' names on **cups.**

57

THESE PLANTS CAN KILL

THE POISON GARDEN

IN NORTH ENGLAND IS A PUBLIC GARDEN FILLED WITH DEADLY PLANTS.

On Christmas Island in the Indian Ocean, **red crabs** outnumber people by about **29,000 to 1.**

FLASHES OF LIGHT SOMETIMES APPEAR IN THE **SKY** BEFORE AND DURING EARTHQUAKES.

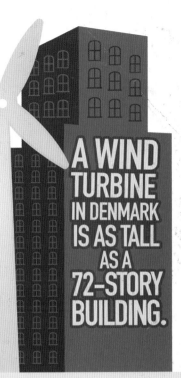

A WIND TURBINE IN DENMARK IS AS TALL AS A 72-STORY BUILDING.

THE ARCHES OF A **McDONALD'S** IN SEDONA, ARIZONA, U.S.A., ARE TURQUOISE INSTEAD OF YELLOW.

A CHOCOLATE BAR NAMED **CHICKEN DINNER** USED TO BE SOLD IN THE UNITED STATES.

Just a **teaspoon** (5 mL) of a **neutron star's matter** would weigh **six billion tons.** (5.5 billion t)

About **50 million** inhabitants of the **United States** don't use the **Internet—** that's more people than the entire population of **Argentina.**

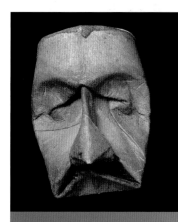

ONE FRENCH ARTIST CREATES **FACE MASKS** USING **TOILET PAPER ROLLS.**

A GROUP OF GOATS

In Japan, you can buy doughnuts stuffed with ramen noodles.

A **POMERANIAN** BECAME THE **FASTEST DOG** ON TWO PAWS AFTER WALKING NEARLY **33 FEET** (10 m) IN LESS THAN SEVEN SECONDS ON HIS **HIND LEGS.**

THE U.S. SUPREME COURT BUILDING IN WASHINGTON, D.C., HAS A BASKETBALL COURT ON ITS TOP FLOOR.

NEW YORK CITY'S NEW YEAR'S EVE BALL IS MADE UP OF **2,688** CRYSTAL PANELS.

A STUDY FOUND THAT BABIES BORN IN WINTER TEND TO CRAWL SOONER THAN BABIES BORN IN SUMMER.

69

A Dutch **artist** created a **69-foot-long** (21-m) **wooden** **hippo** and floated it down London's River Thames.

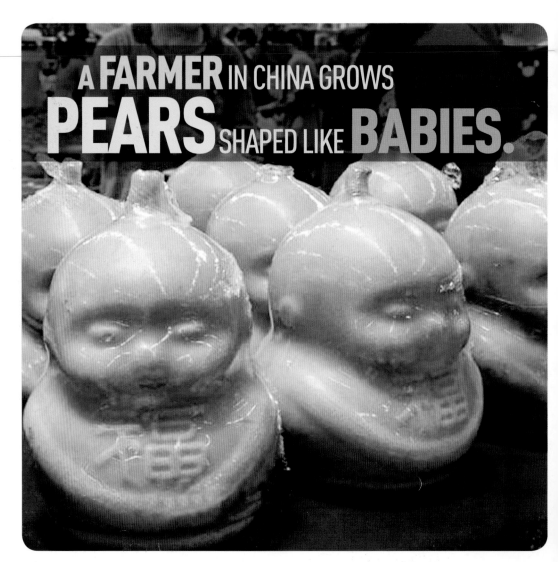

A **FARMER** IN CHINA GROWS **PEARS** SHAPED LIKE **BABIES.**

Restaurant diners *who sit by a window tend to order* **salads** *more often, according to one study.*

Osprey birds *build nests* **big enough** *to fit an* **adult human inside.**

Walt Disney World's *Cinderella* **Castle** contains a *hotel suite* that **sleeps** six people.

A company in the **Middle East** makes bodysuits for camels **to wear** while **training** for races.

THE
**AMAZON
RAIN FOREST**
IS ABOUT TWICE
THE SIZE OF
INDIA.

MORE THAN
**100 MILLION
YEARS AGO,**
INDIA WAS AN
ISLAND.

Male **walruses** make a bell-like sound to **attract mates.**

Some **squat lobsters**—a kind of crustacean—are covered in **hairlike bristles.**

A MAN IN ILLINOIS, U.S.A., **BUILT A PICKUP TRUCK** THAT LOOKS AS IF IT HAS BEEN **FLIPPED** UPSIDE DOWN.

ZUCCHINIS ARE ABOUT 95 PERCENT WATER.

YOU'RE **30 TIMES** MORE LIKELY TO **LAUGH** WHEN YOU'RE AROUND **FRIENDS** THAN WHEN YOU'RE **ALONE!**

Hagfish digest **food** through their **skin.**

Mexico once had **three different presidents** in power in one day.

An **Australian** man set a world record by **drumming 1,553** drumbeats in one minute.

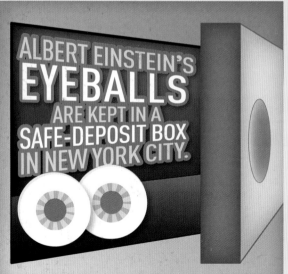

ALBERT EINSTEIN'S **EYEBALLS** ARE KEPT IN A SAFE-DEPOSIT BOX IN NEW YORK CITY.

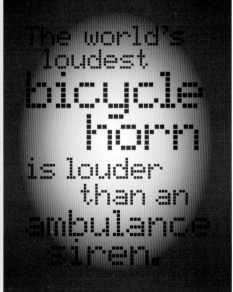

The world's loudest **bicycle horn** is louder than an ambulance siren.

A BEAVER'S IRON-RICH DIET TURNS ITS FRONT TEETH ORANGE.

There are more than 1,000 varieties of mango.

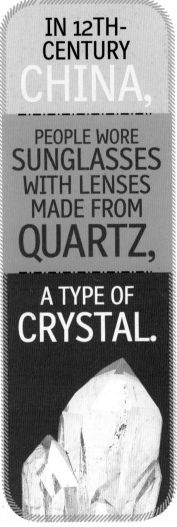

IN 12TH-CENTURY CHINA, PEOPLE WORE SUNGLASSES WITH LENSES MADE FROM QUARTZ, A TYPE OF CRYSTAL.

Australia's **Great Barrier Reef** is roughly the size of **Italy.**

83

A **crosswalk light** in Lisbon, Portugal, features a figure **dancing to music** as the **stop signal.**

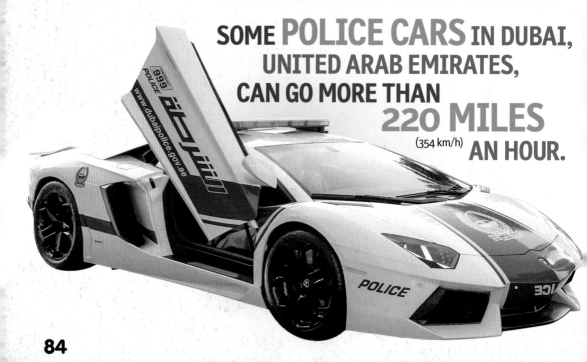

SOME **POLICE CARS** IN DUBAI, UNITED ARAB EMIRATES, CAN GO MORE THAN **220 MILES** (354 km/h) AN HOUR.

THERE ARE FIVE TIMES AS MANY BICYCLES AS CARS IN COPENHAGEN, DENMARK.

IT'S IMPOSSIBLE FOR A **BAT** TO STAND UPRIGHT.

TOGETHER, A
**TARSIER'S
EYES**
WEIGH NEARLY AS
MUCH AS
ITS BRAIN.

As a training tool, the U.S. military
created a plan to
combat zombies.

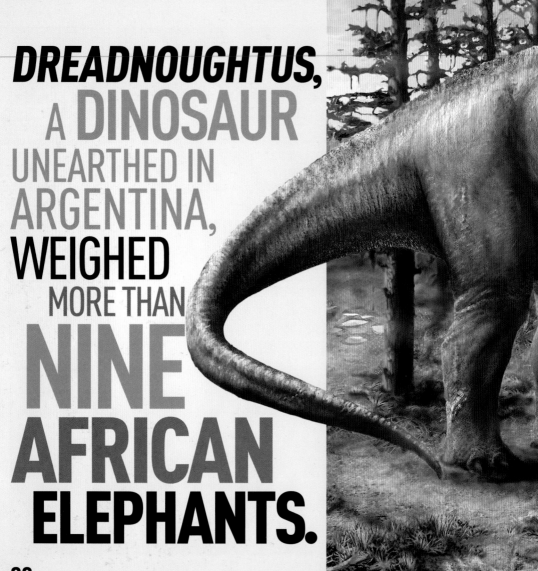

DREADNOUGHTUS, A **DINOSAUR** UNEARTHED IN ARGENTINA, WEIGHED MORE THAN **NINE AFRICAN ELEPHANTS.**

By snapping its **claw**, the pistol shrimp creates a jet of water that can travel **62 miles** (100 km/h) **an hour.**

Roman gladiators consumed an **energy drink** containing ash.

Algae sometimes **grow** on **sloth fur.**

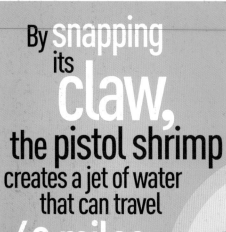

SOME 20 BILLION PLANETS IN OUR GALAXY COULD SUPPORT ALIEN LIFE.

Buttered bread topped with sprinkles is a popular breakfast in the Netherlands.

AN OREGON **MAN** MADE A **40-FOOT-TALL** (12-m) NUTCRACKER THAT CAN **CRACK** COCONUTS.

SCIENTISTS CREATED A **FORK** THAT MEASURES HOW LONG YOU PAUSE BETWEEN BITES TO SHOW *HOW FAST YOU'RE EATING.*

SOME KINDS OF **APPLES** **ARE** **PINK** ON THE INSIDE.

In the 1950s, dyed goat hair was used for miniature golf putting greens.

The first steam **locomotive** made in the United States lost a race to a **horse.**

93

SOME **OLD JETS** ARE PLACED

IN AIRPLANE GRAVEYARDS.

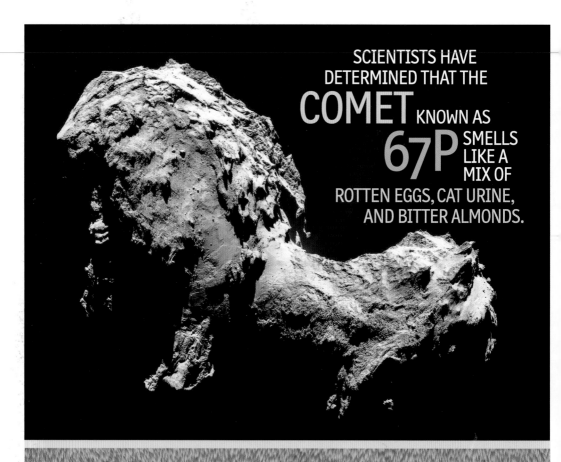

SCIENTISTS HAVE DETERMINED THAT THE COMET KNOWN AS 67P SMELLS LIKE A MIX OF ROTTEN EGGS, CAT URINE, AND BITTER ALMONDS.

CAMELS ARE BORN WITHOUT HUMPS.

HERMIT CRABS COMMUNICATE BY CHIRPING.

Some **snakes** can see the **heat** given off by mammals' **bodies.**

BOXER DOGS SOMETIMES FIGHT BY STANDING ON THEIR **HIND LEGS** AND BATTING EACH OTHER WITH THEIR **FRONT PAWS.**

Some **worms** that live on **coral reefs** look like tiny, colorful **Christmas trees.**

Scientists used a **robot** disguised as a **penguin** to study real **emperor penguins.**

Candidates named **Darth Vader** and **Master Yoda** have run for office in Ukraine.

THE LANGUAGE OF THE EWOKS IN *RETURN OF THE JEDI*

100

A MAN BUILT **A DRONE** THAT LOOKS LIKE HAN SOLO'S SHIP, THE **MILLENNIUM FALCON.**

IS PARTLY BASED ON TIBETAN AND NEPALI.

IN 1921,

NEARLY

76

INCHES
(193 cm)
OF SNOW

FELL IN
24 HOURS
ON SILVER LAKE,
COLORADO, U.S.A.

One
volcano in
Indonesia burns
with **electric-blue
flames.**

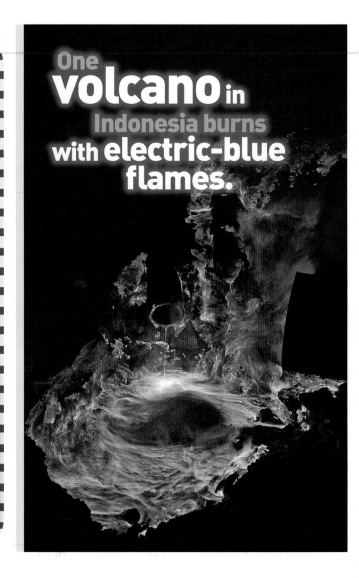

The Super Soaker **water gun** was originally called the **Power** Drencher.

EVERY DAY 100 TONS OF (91 t) **COSMIC DUST** FROM SPACE ENTERS EARTH'S ATMOSPHERE— THAT'S THE SAME WEIGHT AS **400 MOUNTAIN GORILLAS.**

HERDS OF **BUFFALO-SIZE** RODENTS ONCE ROAMED SOUTH AMERICA.

HONEYPOT WORKER ANTS,
WHICH STORE NECTAR IN THEIR BODIES, CAN SWELL TO THE SIZE OF A GRAPE.

Shoppers are more likely to buy a product if they touch it, one study found.

The name **Crayola** is a combination of two French words that together mean "oily chalk."

THE TEETH OF AT LEAST TWO SHARK SPECIES ARE NATURALLY COATED IN FLUORIDE, A MAIN INGREDIENT IN TOOTHPASTE.

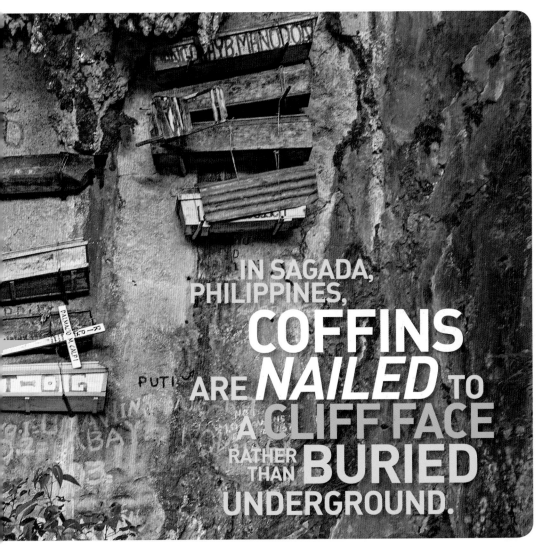

IN SAGADA, PHILIPPINES, **COFFINS** ARE *NAILED* TO A CLIFF FACE RATHER THAN **BURIED** UNDERGROUND.

CUCUMBERS WERE KNOWN AS "COWCUMBERS" UNTIL THE MID-19TH CENTURY.

LOUISIANA, U.S.A., IS HOME TO SOME **500,000** WILD PIGS.

A
New York City
artist invented a
waffle iron
that makes
waffles
shaped like a
computer keyboard.

COFFEE WITH **CREAM** STAYS **HOTTER** LONGER THAN PLAIN **BLACK** COFFEE.

AS
A HEN
GETS OLDER,
SHE PRODUCES
BIGGER
EGGS.

THE INTERNATIONAL SPACE STATION WEIGHS MORE THAN 300 CARS.

A WARM GOLF BALL WILL TRAVEL FARTHER THROUGH THE AIR THAN A COLD ONE.

Every year, **300 million golf balls** are lost or thrown away in the United States.

GOLF WAS BANNED IN 15TH-CENTURY SCOTLAND.

ONE KIND OF MITE CAN SPRINT 20 TIMES FASTER THAN A CHEETAH, AS MEASURED IN BODY LENGTHS TRAVELED EACH SECOND.

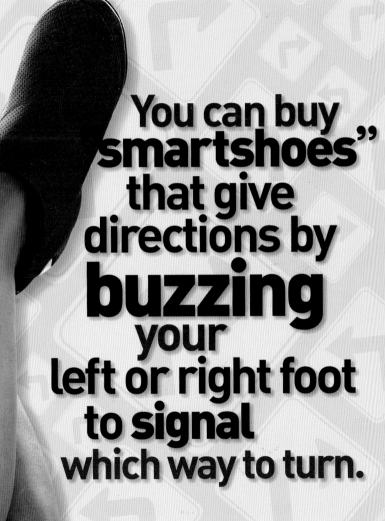

You can buy **smartshoes"** that give directions by **buzzing** your left or right foot to **signal** which way to turn.

IT WOULD TAKE ABOUT **TEN STACKED EMPIRE STATE BUILDINGS** TO STRETCH FROM THE GULF OF MEXICO'S DEEPEST POINT TO ITS SURFACE.

Crocodiles sometimes climb trees.

118

ONE TYPE OF **OWL** IN **AUSTRALIA BARKS LIKE A DOG.**

ICE SCULPTORS IN TEXAS, U.S.A., RE-CREATED SCENES FROM *FROSTY THE SNOWMAN* USING **2 MILLION POUNDS** (907,185 kg) **OF ICE.**

Grasshopper Glacier in Montana, U.S.A., contains layers of **grasshoppers** preserved in ice.

Certain **radio signals** coming from **Jupiter** sound like **popcorn popping.**

120

OVER **40** PERCENT OF **AMERICANS**

HAVE **ANCESTORS** WHO FIRST ENTERED **THE UNITED STATES**

THROUGH **ELLIS ISLAND** IN **NEW YORK BAY.**

1904

CURIOUS GEORGE WAS ORIGINALLY NAMED FIFI.

SCIENTISTS LANDED A REMOTE-CONTROLLED SPACECRAFT ON A COMET THAT WAS TRAVELING **84,000 MILES** (135,185 km/h) AN HOUR.

MOUNTAIN LIONS HAVE EXTRA-LARGE **TASTE BUDS** ON THEIR TONGUES THAT HELP SCRAPE **MEAT** FROM BONES.

The *cruise ship* Queen Mary 2 *has a plant that makes* freshwater *from* saltwater.

The average car has some 25,000 parts.

THE CREATOR OF WONDER WOMAN

ALSO INVENTED AN EARLY VERSION OF THE LIE DETECTOR.

123

IT TOOK THE INVENTOR OF THE **RUBIK'S CUBE** MORE THAN A **MONTH TO SOLVE THE PUZZLE** AFTER SCRAMBLING IT FOR THE FIRST TIME.

THE WORLD'S **LARGEST RUBIK'S CUBE** IS 17-BY-17-BY-17 CUBES.

125

Some **streets** in Seattle, Washington, U.S.A., **boast** **artwork** that only becomes **visible** when splashed with **water.**

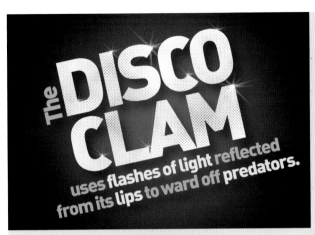

The DISCO CLAM uses flashes of light reflected from its lips to ward off predators.

No cars are allowed on **Sark Island** in the **English Channel.**

IF BUNDLED TOGETHER, ALL THE BRANCHES OF A TREE WOULD BE ABOUT AS THICK AS ITS TRUNK.

THE AVERAGE PENCIL HAS ENOUGH GRAPHITE

MOOSE
are also called
RUBBER-NOSED
swamp donkeys.

Cashew nuts
and poison ivy
are closely related.

AFRICA'S NILE RIVER IS LONGER THAN THE

TO DRAW A LINE THAT'S 35 MILES LONG.

(56 km)

The
Tinkerbell wasp
is only **two and a half times**
the width of a **human hair.**

WIDTH OF THE CONTIGUOUS **UNITED STATES.**

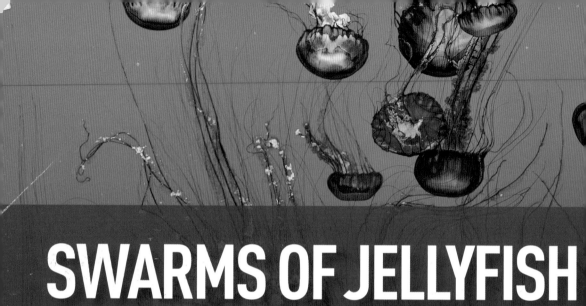

SWARMS OF JELLYFISH HAVE APPEARED IN

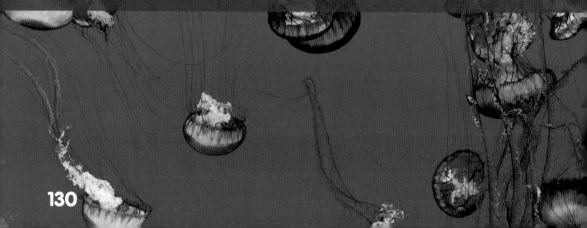

(161 km)

STRETCHING 100 MILES
THE GULF OF MEXICO.

THE **DIVING BELL SPIDER** IS THE ONLY SPIDER THAT LIVES ITS **LIFE** ENTIRELY **UNDERWATER.**

THE PLANET KEPLER-413B WOBBLES LIKE A *SPINNING TOP.*

A study found that saying "**OW**" can help you tolerate pain better.

THE EIFFEL TOWER "GROWS" ABOUT SIX INCHES TALLER IN SUMMER, WHEN THE HEAT MAKES ITS IRON EXPAND.

(15 cm)

SEVERAL **CAVES** IN KENTUCKY, U.S.A., ARE HOME TO A SPECIES OF SEE-THROUGH, **EYELESS SHRIMP.**

Canadians eat more doughnuts than any other country's citizens.

NASA'S HUBBLE TELESCOPE CAPTURED AN IMAGE OF A GALAXY CLUSTER THAT LOOKS LIKE A SMILEY FACE.

THE **POLICE SQUAD** OF ONE SOUTHERN **RUSSIAN TOWN** IS MADE UP ENTIRELY OF **IDENTICAL TWINS** AND **TRIPLETS.**

You can **cycle** down a **glow-in-the-dark bike path** in the **Netherlands.**

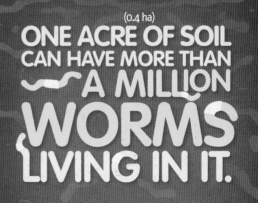

MORE THAN **100 MILES** (161 km) OF **MINING TUNNELS** EXIST UNDER DETROIT, MICHIGAN, U.S.A.

(0.4 ha) ONE ACRE OF SOIL CAN HAVE MORE THAN A MILLION **WORMS** LIVING IN IT.

Google used a *camel with a camera* mounted on its hump to help map a desert *in the* United Arab Emirates.

SPRAY FROM AFRICA'S VICTORIA FALLS CAN SHOOT 1,600 FEET IN THE AIR.

(500 m)

To distribute **berries,** **cedar waxwing** **birds** line up and pass them from **beak to beak.**

MALE EMEI MUSTACHE TOADS GROW **A LINE OF SPIKES** ALONG THEIR **UPPER LIPS.**

138

ANCIENT HAWAIIANS SOMETIMES MADE LEIS OUT OF BONES.

EMPEROR PENGUINS CAN'T TASTE THE FISH THEY EAT.

Inventors used a **3-D printer** to produce a working electric car.

MARINE SNAILS' TEETH ARE THE STRONGEST MATERIAL FOUND IN NATURE.

Caribou release an odor from their **ankles** when threatened.

A more than **500-year-old bed** that may have belonged to **King Henry VII** was recently found in a **parking lot** in England.

About one-quarter of the world's hazelnut supply is used to make Nutella.

You can buy a guitar pick made from a meteorite.

In the United States, more than **20 million tons of salt** (18 million t) are spread on snowy roads, parking lots, sidewalks, and driveways each year.

A double somersault with a TWIST performed on a trampoline is called a fliffis.

Scientists think that **sperm whales** can detect a **swimmer** more than **one mile** above them. (1.6 km)

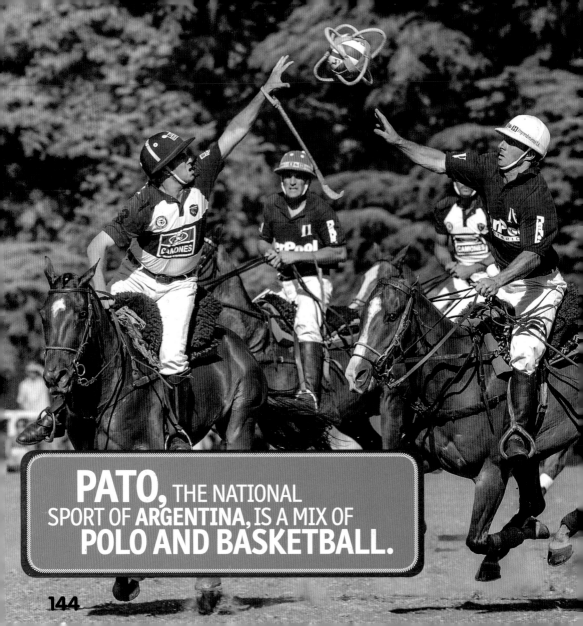

PATO, THE NATIONAL SPORT OF **ARGENTINA,** IS A MIX OF **POLO AND BASKETBALL.**

The average person can recognize about a trillion smells.

Elizabeth II, Queen of England, served as a mechanic in World War II.

The @ symbol is almost five centuries old.

The *Titanic* was held together by 3 million rivets.

CALIFORNIA INVENTORS CREATED

A REAL-LIFE HOVERBOARD.

HENDO

WATCHING FISH SWIM IN AN AQUARIUM CAN REDUCE STRESS, A STUDY FOUND.

Electric eels can use jolts of electricity to control the muscle movements of the fish they hunt.

147

YORKSHIRE TERRIER + POODLE

YORKIPOO

THE ISLAND OF MAURITIUS IN THE INDIAN OCEAN HAS MULTICOLORED SAND DUNES.

IN 1808, TWO FRENCHMEN **FOUGHT A DUEL** WHILE FLOATING IN BALLOONS SOME **2,700 FEET** (820 m) ABOVE GROUND.

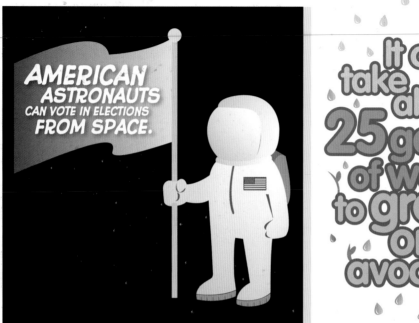

AMERICAN ASTRONAUTS *CAN VOTE IN ELECTIONS* **FROM SPACE.**

It can take about **25 gallons of water** (95 L) to grow one avocado.

The noises **Tasmanian devils** make when eating can be heard **a mile away.** (1.6 km)

THE DESERT-DWELLING **FENNEC FOX HAS HAIRY FOOTPADS** THAT PROTECT ITS FEET FROM HOT SAND.

U.S. FAMILIES SPEND MORE THAN $8 BILLION ON BACK-TO-SCHOOL CLOTHES.

President Gerald Ford once worked as a park ranger.

THAT'S FIN-TASTIC!

A GROUP OF SHARKS

IS CALLED A SHIVER.

YOU CAN SEE **TRACTOR SQUARE DANCES**—WHERE **FARMERS** MANEUVER TRACTORS TO MIMIC SQUARE DANCING ROUTINES— IN THE MIDWESTERN UNITED STATES.

PEOPLE WHO ARE FREQUENTLY **HUGGED** EXPERIENCE LESS SEVERE **COLD** SYMPTOMS, A STUDY FOUND.

Someone who plays **marbles** is called a **mibster**.

156

A HAMSTER'S CHEEK POUCHES EXTEND ALL THE WAY TO ITS hips.

SOME **BOWHEAD WHALES** LIVE FOR MORE THAN **200** YEARS.

157

APPLES CAN RIPEN TEN TIMES FASTER AT ROOM TEMPERATURE THAN IN THE REFRIGERATOR.

AT AN OPERA HOUSE ON THE U.S.–CANADIAN BORDER, THE STAGE IS IN CANADA WHILE MOST SEATS ARE IN THE UNITED STATES.

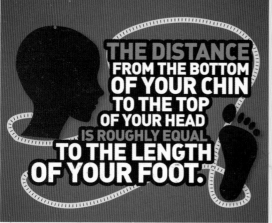

THE DISTANCE FROM THE BOTTOM OF YOUR CHIN TO THE TOP OF YOUR HEAD IS ROUGHLY EQUAL TO THE LENGTH OF YOUR FOOT.

158

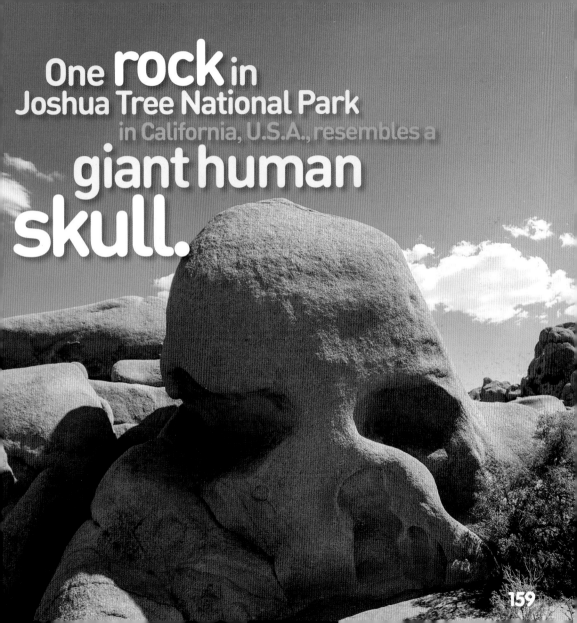

One **rock** in Joshua Tree National Park in California, U.S.A., resembles a giant human skull.

A MALE RED DEER'S ANTLERS CAN GROW

TO A WEIGHT OF 60 POUNDS (27 kg) IN THREE MONTHS.

Six of the seven dwarfs in the 1937 animated movie *Snow White and the Seven Dwarfs* have eyebrows modeled after Walt Disney's.

Temperatures on Mercury can drop more than **1000°F (550°C)** in one day.

A PENNY ISSUED BY THE U.S. MINT IN 1793 SOLD AT AUCTION FOR $2.3 MILLION.

The first baseball **caps** were made from **straw.**

163

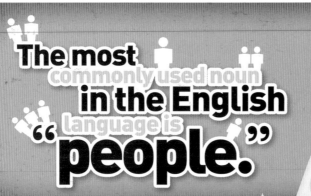

The most commonly used noun **in the English** language is **"people."**

Pelicans can hold more food in their beaks than in their stomachs.

Extreme athletes have skied from the summit of Mount Everest to a base camp 12,000 feet below.

(3,660 m)

ONE ARTIST PAINTED A PICTURE OF BASKETBALL PLAYER **YAO MING,** USING A **BASKETBALL** AS A **"PAINTBRUSH."**

Laid end to end, New York City's subway tracks would stretch from the **Big Apple** to Chicago, Illinois, U.S.A.

YOU CAN FIND OVER

2,000
ROCK
ARCHES
IN **ARCHES**
NATIONAL PARK,

IN UTAH, U.S.A.

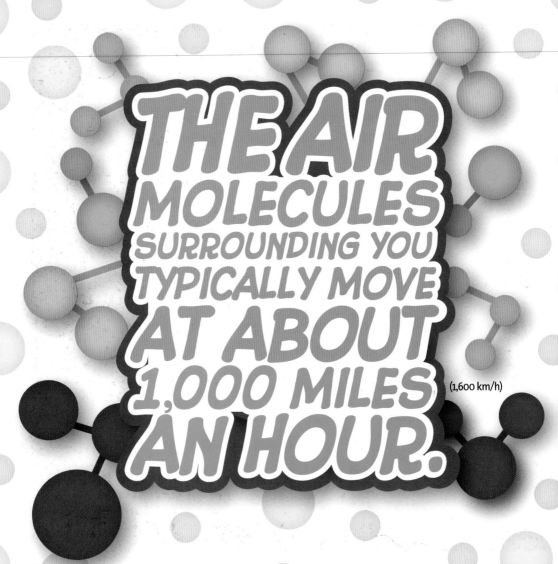

THE AIR MOLECULES SURROUNDING YOU TYPICALLY MOVE AT ABOUT 1,000 MILES AN HOUR. (1,600 km/h)

BOTTLENOSE DOLPHINS SWALLOW THEIR **FOOD WHOLE.**

IN JAPAN, KFC GAVE AWAY iPHONE CASES SHAPED LIKE GIANT CHICKEN DRUMSTICKS.

More than 2 million **GOOGLE** searches happen every minute.

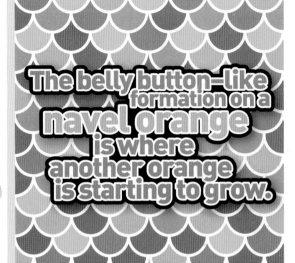

The belly button–like formation on a **navel orange** is where another orange is starting to grow.

PARROTS DON'T HAVE VOCAL CORDS.

A newborn sea otter's extra-thick fur traps in so much air that it's impossible for the animal to sink.

173

SOME **SOCCER BALLS** HAVE A BUILT-IN **CHIP** THAT SIGNALS REFEREES WHEN THE BALL PASSES THE **GOAL LINE.**

3,240 SOCCER BALLS WERE USED DURING THE 2014 WORLD CUP.

PROFESSIONAL **SOCCER PLAYERS** RUN AN AVERAGE OF SEVEN MILES DURING EACH (11 km) **GAME.**

AN INDOOR **SOCCER MATCH** IN ALBERTA, CANADA, LASTED **30 HOURS** AND **10 MINUTES.**

AN ATLANTIC PUFFIN CAN HOLD AS MANY AS A DOZEN SMALL FISH IN ITS BILL AT ONE TIME.

SOME MOTHS DON'T HAVE MOUTHS.

175

Pippi Longstocking's full name is Pippilotta Delicatessa Windowshade Mackrelmint Ephraim's Daughter Longstocking.

Watermelon *seeds* *were found in* **King Tut's tomb.**

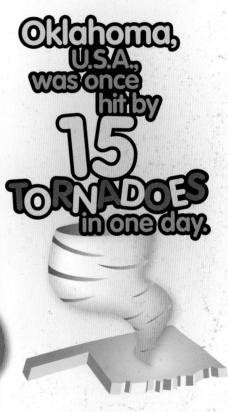

Oklahoma, U.S.A., was once hit by **15 TORNADOES** in one day.

AN **ARTiST** IN LONDON, ENGLAND, CONSTRUCTED A **BUiLDiNG** THAT **APPEARS** TO **LEViTATE.**

A HEDGEHOG HAS ABOUT

6,000 QUILLS.

Polar bears sometimes communicate by touching noses.

SOME PEOPLE **LACK** THE GENE THAT CAUSES **SMELLY** UNDERARMS.

ONIONS AND **GARLIC** CAN BE USED TO HELP SOAK UP TOXIC SPILLS.

TRISKAIDEKAPHOBIA IS THE FEAR OF THE NUMBER 13.

THE WORLD'S LARGEST **DISCO BALL** IS MORE THAN **33 FEET** (10 m) IN DIAMETER—ALMOST AS WIDE AS A TENNIS COURT

The common **octopus** is the size of a **flea** at birth.

INK FROM THE COMMON **OCTOPUS** CONTAINS A SUBSTANCE THAT DULLS A PREDATOR'S SENSE OF **SMELL.**

SOME **OCTOPUSES** BUILD FORTRESSES OUT OF **SHELLS AND ROCKS.**

You can buy Thanksgiving-themed **gumballs** with flavors such as cranberry, turkey, and pumpkin pie.

SOME **21,000** YEARS AGO, MASSIVE **ICEBERGS** FLOATED OFF THE COAST OF FLORIDA, U.S.A.

Scientists have figured out a way to convert **sugar** into **fuel.**

India sent a spacecraft known as MOM to Mars.

Researchers are trying to develop a car tire made from dandelions.

MOST SHARKS WOULD SINK IN FRESHWATER.

More than **1,400** varieties of cheese exist in the world.

CERTAIN FERNS EJECT THEIR SPORES WITH A CATAPULT MOTION.

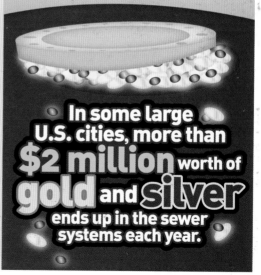

In some large U.S. cities, more than **$2 million** worth of **gold** and **silver** ends up in the sewer systems each year.

A GROUP OF GIRAFFES

WONDER HOW WE GOT THAT NAME?

IS CALLED A TOWER.

A West Indian manatee's **lungs** are two-thirds the length of its body.

Your glabella is the area of skin between your eyebrows.

IN 2014,
TWO PROFESSORS
LIVED FOR

73 DAYS
IN AN

AIRTIGHT
LODGE

ABOUT (7.6 m)
25 FEET
UNDERWATER

OFF THE COAST OF
FLORIDA, U.S.A.

All of
Earth's
land
could fit in the
Pacific
Ocean.

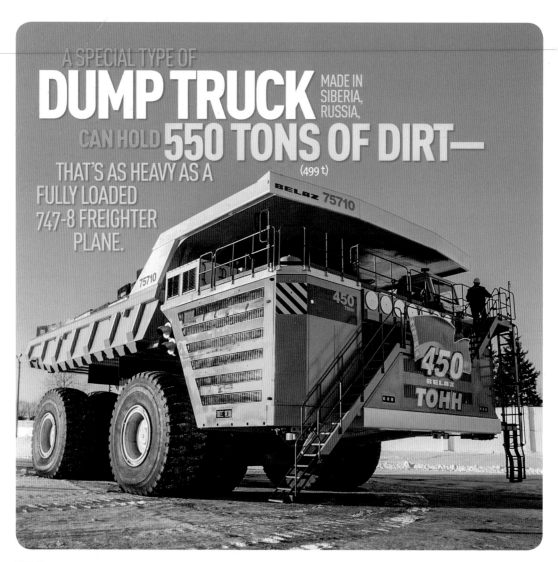

A SPECIAL TYPE OF

DUMP TRUCK MADE IN SIBERIA, RUSSIA,

CAN HOLD **550 TONS OF DIRT—**
(499 t)

THAT'S AS HEAVY AS A FULLY LOADED 747-8 FREIGHTER PLANE.

The American **goldfinch** sometimes sounds as if it's saying **"po-tay-toe-chip"** when it chirps.

WAVES OFF THE COAST OF PUERTO MALABRIGO, PERU, CAN STRETCH MORE THAN A **MILE LONG.**
(1.6 km)

A SINGLE BANANA IS CALLED A FINGER; A BUNCH IS CALLED **A HAND.**

MALE **KANGAROOS** **FLEX** THEIR BICEPS TO **IMPRESS** FEMALES.

ENOUGH **CANDY CORN** IS MADE EVERY YEAR TO GIVE EVERY PERSON ON EARTH ONE KERNEL.

89 PERCENT OF PEOPLE EAT A CHOCOLATE

FACTFINDER

Boldface indicates illustrations.

Staff for This Book
Andrea Silen, *Project Editor*
Julide Dengel, *Art Director*
Hillary Leo, *Photo Editor*
Paige Towler, *Editorial Assistant*
Sanjida Rashid and Rachel Kenny, *Design Production Assistants*
Michael Cassady and Mari Robinson, *Rights Clearance Specialists*
Grace Hill, *Managing Editor*
Joan Gossett, *Senior Production Editor*
Lewis R. Bassford, *Production Manager*
Nicole Elliott, *Manager, Production Services*
Susan Borke, *Legal and Business Affairs*
John Chow, *Imaging*

Senior Management Team, Kids Publishing and Media
Nancy Laties Feresten, *Senior Vice President*; Erica Green, *Vice President, Editorial Director, Kids Books*; Julie Vosburgh Agnone, *Vice President, Operations*; Jennifer Emmett, *Vice President, Content*; Michelle Sullivan, *Vice President, Video and Digital Initiatives*; Eva Absher-Schantz, *Vice President, Visual Identity*; Rachel Buchholz, *Editor and Vice President*, NG Kids *magazine*; Jay Sumner, *Photo Director*; Hannah August, *Marketing Director*; R. Gary Colbert, *Production Director*

Digital
Laura Goertzel, *Manager*; Sara Zeglin, *Senior Producer*; Bianca Bowman, *Assistant Producer*; Natalie Jones, *Senior Product Manager*

Since 1888, the National Geographic Society has funded more than 12,000 research, exploration, and preservation projects around the world. The Society receives funds from National Geographic Partners, LLC, funded in part by your purchase. A portion of the proceeds from this book supports this vital work. To learn more, visit www.natgeo.com/info.

NATIONAL GEOGRAPHIC and Yellow Border Design are trademarks of the National Geographic Society, used under license.

For more information, please visit nationalgeographic.com, call 1-800-647-5463, or write to the following address:
National Geographic Partners
1145 17th Street N.W.
Washington, DC 20036-4688 U.S.A.

Visit us online at nationalgeographic.com/books

For librarians and teachers: ngchildrensbooks.org

More for kids from National Geographic:
kids.nationalgeographic.com

For information about special discounts for bulk purchases, please contact National Geographic Books Special Sales: ngspecsales@ngs.org

For rights or permissions inquiries, please contact National Geographic Books Subsidiary Rights: ngbookrights@ngs.org

Paperback ISBN: 978-1-4263-2086-6
Reinforced library binding ISBN: 978-1-4263-2087-3

Printed in China
16/PPS/2

Time to go from WEIRD to WOO-HOO!

This giant boredom-buster is full of awesome games, brain-tickling quizzes, laugh-out-loud jokes, puzzles, mazes, and tons more fun.

NATIONAL GEOGRAPHIC KiDS

SMART FUN!

Boredom-BUSTING Fun Stuff

COOL GAMES

HILARIOUS JOKES

NO WAY

AWESOME QUIZZES

AND MORE!

RAIN FOREST ROUNDUP
These photographs show close-up views of animals that live in the rain forest. Unscramble the letters to identify what's in each picture.
Bonus: Use the highlighted letters to solve the puzzle below.

ABT

OSRL

PREVI

ARPHNIA

EROP

RAPT

OATNCU

Just Joking

Q What do you feed a noisy dog?

A Hush puppies.

Porcupines can grow new quills to replace the ones that fall out.

What did the **porcupine** say to the **cactus**?

Just you, Mommy?

Q What did the banana do when the monkey chased it?

Q Why did the watchmaker enjoy his vacation?